French Holidav Cool

Camping Lite

Liz Garnett

Beechthorpe Press

First published in 2017 by Beechthorpe Press
Copyright © Liz Garnett
www.lizgarnett.com
Photography credits: Liz Garnett

ISBN: 978-0-9935603-2-3

CONTENTS

Notes for the reader

In order to take as few utensils as possible most ingredients are measured using measuring spoons or measuring cups. Where measurements are in kilograms or grams it is assumed that these will be measured at the market or supermarket.

SALADS

Salad Dressings

Lemon and Olive Oil
2 tbsps olive oil (l'huile d'olive)
juice of 1 lemon (le citron)

Oil and Vinegar
2 tbsps olive oil (l'huile d'olive)
1 tbsp balsamic vinegar (le vinaigre balsamique)

Salad Dressing
2 tbsps olive oil (l'huile d'olive)
1 tsp mustard (le moutarde)
1 tbsp balsamic vinegar (le vinaigre balsamique)

Chilli Salad Dressing
2 tbsps olive oil (l'huile d'olive)
1 tsp mustard (le moutarde)
1 tbsp lime juice (le citron vert)
1 tsp honey (le miel)
1 small chilli (le piment rouge), finely chopped

Honey and Lemon Vinaigrette
1 tbsp lemon juice (le citron)
1 tbsp honey (le miel)
2 tbsps olive oil (l'huile d'olive)

Egg Salad with Asparagus and Lardons

Serves 2

Ingredients
2 hard boiled egg (l'oeuf), peeled and sliced
bunch of asparagus (l'asperges), cooked
100g lardons, cooked
2 tbsps olive oil (l'huile d'olive)
1 tbsp balsamic vinegar (le vinaigre balsamique)
1 clove garlic (l'ail), crushed
1 tsp dijon mustard (le moutarde)

Instructions
- Arrange asparagus on two plates and place egg slices on top of asparagus.
- Mix olive oil, balsamic vinegar, garlic and mustard and pour over asparagus and eggs.
- Sprinkle lardons over eggs and asparagus.
- Serve.

Alternatives
- Replace lardons with chopped smoked salmon pieces.
- Replace lardons with 4 anchovy fillets.

Beetroot Salad with Capers

Serves 2

Ingredient

1 medium beetroot (la betterave rouge), grated raw
3 tbsps capers (la câpre), chopped
2 tbsps olive oil (l'huile d'olive)
2 tbsps lemon juice (le citron)
75g soft goats cheese (le chèvre frais), crumbled
1 small lettuce (la laiture)

Instructions

- Line the bottom of a large bowl with lettuce leaves.
- Combine beetroot, capers, olive oil and lemon juice and pile on top of lettuce.
- Crumble goats cheese on top of beetroot.
- Serve.

Potato Salad with Fennel and Celery

Serves 2

Ingredients

300g new potatoes (la pomme de terre), thickly sliced
100g lardons
2 sticks celery (le céleri-en-branche), finely sliced
1 small bulb fennel (le feneuil), finely sliced
1 tbsp lemon juice (le citron)
1 tbsp olive oil (l'huile d'olive)
1 tsp honey (le miel)

Instructions

- Cook new potatoes until tender.
- Fry lardons without oil until crispy. Remove lardons and put to one side.
- Combine potatoes, lardons, celery and fennel.
- Mix lemon juice, olive oil and honey and pour over salad.
- Serve.

Potato Salad

Serves 2

Ingredients

300g new potatoes (la pomme de terre)

½ cucumber (le conconbre), cubed

1 little gem lettuce (la laiture), torn

2 tbsps olive oil (l'huile d'olive)

2 tbsps capers (la câpre)

1 tbsp lemon (le citron)

1 tbsp fresh thyme (le thym), finely chopped

Instructions

- Boil potatoes and leave to cool.
- Combine all the ingredients in a bowl and mix well.
- Serve.

Kholrabi Salad

Serves 2

Ingredients

1 kholrabi (le chou-rave), sliced finely into matchsticks
1 apple (la pomme), diced
1 little gem lettuce (la laiture), torn
handful of pine nuts (le pignon de pin)
2 tbsps lemon juice (le citron)
½ tsp honey (le miel)
½ tsp dijon mustard (le moutarde)
2 tbsps olive oil (l'huile d'olive)

Instructions

- Combine kholrabi, apple and pine nuts in a large bowl.
- Mix lemon juice, honey, mustard and olive oil and pour over salad and mix well.
- Serve.

Celeriac Rémoulade

Serves 2

Ingredients

3 tbsp good quality mayonnaise (la mayonnaise)
1 tbsp Dijon mustard (le moutarde)
Juice of 1 lemon (le citron)
1 small celeriac (le céleri-rave), peeled and grated
Salt and pepper (le sel et le poivre)

Instructions

- Mix mayonnaise, mustard and lemon juice in a large bowl.
- Add the grated celeriac and mix well.
- Serve.

Beetroot Coleslaw

Serves 2

Ingredients

1 small carrot (la carotte), grated

1 small raw beetroot (la betterave rouge), grated

⅛ red cabbage (le chou rouge), finely sliced

1 apple (la pomme), grated

1 tbsp olive oil (l'huile d'olive)

2 tbsps lemon juice (le citron)

1 tsp honey (le miel)

Handful of pinenuts (le pignon de pin)

Instructions

- Combine lemon juice, olive oil, and honey in a large bowl.
- Add the rest of the ingredients and stir well.
- Serve.

Fennel Coleslaw

Serves 2

Ingredients

1 small bulb fennel (le feneuil), finely sliced
1 green apple (la pomme), cored and finely sliced
1 carrot (la carotte), grated
1 stick celery (le céleri-en-branche), finely sliced
2 tbsps mayonnaise (la mayonnaise)
2 tbsps lemon juice (le citron)

Instructions

- Combine fennel, apple, carrot, and celery in a bowl.
- Mix mayonnaise and lemon juice and add to the vegetables and stir well.
- Serve.

Red Cabbage Coleslaw

Serves 2

Ingredients

½ a small red cabbage (le chou rouge), finely sliced
1 carrot (la carotte), grated
1 small red onion (l'oignon rouge), finely chopped
½ red chilli (le piment rouge), finely chopped
2 tbsps mayonnaise (la mayonnaise)
2 tbsps lime juice (le citron vert)

Instructions

- Mix mayonnaise and lime juice.
- Combine cabbage, carrot, onion and chilli in a large bowl.
- Pour the dressing over the vegetables and mix well.
- Serve.

Celeriac Coleslaw

Serves 2

Ingredients

1 tbsp honey (le miel)
½ tsp Dijon mustard (le moutarde)
Juice 1 lemon (le citron)
2 tbsps olive oil (l'huile d'olive)
1 small celeriac (le céleri-rave), peeled and cut into matchsticks
1 apple (la pomme), cored and finely sliced
¼ small red cabbage (le chou rouge), finely sliced
½ cup pinenuts (le pignon de pin)
1 handful fresh parsley (le persil), chopped
Salt and pepper (le sel et le poivre)

Instructions

- Mix honey, mustard, lemon juice and olive oil. Pour into a large bowl.
- Add celeriac, apple and cabbage to the bowl and mix well.
- Add pinenuts and parsley.
- Mix and serve.

PASTA / RICE / COUSCOUS / QUINOA

Basic Pasta Sauces ... 18

Mediterranean Couscous ... 19

Quinoa, Watercress and Goats Cheese Salad ... 20

Quinoa, Avocado and Radish Salad ... 21

Quinoa and Mozarella Salad ... 22

Quinoa, Prawn and Grapefruit Salad ... 23

Pasta with Broad Beans and Smoked Salmon ... 24

Pasta with Clams ... 25

Creamy Ham Pasta ... 26

Pasta with Artichokes and Peas ... 27

Leek and Lardon Risotto ... 28

Scallop and Prawn Risotto ... 29

Asparagus and Lemon Risotto ... 30

Basic Pasta Sauces

Fresh Tomato Sauce

1 tbsp olive oil (l'huile d'olive) / 1 clove garlic (l'ail), crushed / 400g cherry tomatoes (la tomate cerise), halved / 2 cups fresh basil (le basilica), chopped

- Put tomatoes in boiling water for 2 minutes, remove from water and peel.
- Heat oil in a large frying pan, add garlic and cook for 2 minutes.
- Add cherry tomatoes and cook until it becomes a sauce. Add water or wine if it is becoming too dry.
- Add further ingredients of your choice and cook.
- Add basil.
- Add cooked pasta and stir.
- Serve with fresh parmesan.

Garlic and Chilli Sauce

3 tbsps olive oil (l'huile d'olive) / 2 cloves garlic (l'ail), finely chopped / 1 red chilli (le piment rouge), finely chopped / 2 tbsps fresh parsley (le persil), finely chopped

- Heat oil in a pan and cook garlic and chilli over a gentle heat until softened.
- Add further ingredients of your choice.
- Add cooked pasta and sprinkle with parsley and serve with fresh parmesan.

Mediterranean Couscous

Serves 2

Ingredients

½ cup couscous (le couscous)

250g cherry tomatoes (la tomate cerise), halved

½ cucumber (le concombre), finely diced

11 radishes (le radis), finely sliced

handful fresh parsley (le persil), chopped

½ cup greek yoghurt (le yaourt à la Grecque nature)

2 tbsps lemon juice (le citron)

1 clove garlic (l'ail), crushed

Instructions

- Put couscous in a bowl and pour over with ¾ cup of boiling water, cover and leave to cool.
- Combine couscous, tomatoes, cucumber, radishes and parsley in a large bowl.
- Mix yoghurt, lemon juice and garlic and pour over salad.
- Mix well.
- Serve.

Quinoa, Watercress and Goats Cheese Salad

Serves 2

Ingredients
¼ cup quinoa (le quinoa)
1 small red onion (l'oignon rouge), finely chopped
1 tbsp olive oil (l'huile d'olive)
1 tbsp balsamic vinegar (le vinaigre balsamique)
150g cherry tomatoes (la tomate cerise), halved
Handful of watercress (le cresson), torn
10 large green olives (l'olive), sliced
1 tbsp capers (la câpre)
¼ cup pine nuts (le pignon de pin)
75g firm goats cheese (le fromage de chèvre), crumbled or feta?

Instructions
- Cook quinoa for 15 minutes in boiling water, drain and leave to cool.
- Combine onion, olive oil, balsamic vinegar, tomatoes, watercress, olives, capers, quinoa and pine nuts in a bowl.
- Mix well.
- Crumble goats cheese on top of salad.
- Serve.

Quinoa, Avocado and Radish Salad

Serves 2

Ingredients
¼ cup quinoa (le quinoa)
1 cup fresh broad beans (les féves), cooked
1 small avocado (l'avocat), chopped
handful radishes (le radis), sliced
½ cup fresh basil (le basilica), chopped
2 tbsps lemon juice (le citron)
2 tbsps olive oil (l'huile d'olive)
1 clove garlic (l'ail), crushed

Instructions
- Cook quinoa for 15 minutes in boiling water, drain and leave to cool.
- Combine quinoa, broad beans, avocado, radishes and basil in a large bowl.
- Mix lemon juice, olive oil and garlic and pour over salad.
- Serve.

Quinoa and Mozarella Salad

Serves 2

Ingredients

¼ cup dried quinoa (le quinoa)

1 small red onion (l'oignon rouge), finely chopped

½ courgette (la courgette), finely cubed

4 sundried tomatoes (la tomate sechée), roughly chopped

1 red pepper (le poivron rouge), chargrilled and sliced

1 mozarella, cubed

2 tbsps lemon juice (le citron)

2 tbsps olive oil (l'huile d'olive)

1 clove garlic (l'ail), crushed

Instructions

- Cook quinoa for 15 minutes in boiling water, drain and leave to cool.
- Combine, quinoa, onion, courgette, tomatoes, red pepper and mozzarella in a large bowl.
- Mix lemon juice, olive oil and crushed garlic and pour over salad.
- Mix well.
- Serve with bread and cold meats.

Quinoa, Prawn and Grapefruit Salad

Serves 2

Ingredients

½ cup quinoa (le quinoa)

1 red grapefruit (le pamplemouse), segmented and reserve juice

1 avocado (l'avocat), sliced

200g prawns (la crevette), cooked

2 handfuls toasted pinenuts (le pignon de pin)

1 handful parsley (le persil), chopped

2 tbsps olive oil (l'huile d'olive)

2 tsps honey (le miel)

Instructions

- Cook quinoa in boiling water for 15 minutes, drain and leave to cool.
- Combine quinoa, grapefruit, avocado, prawns, pinenuts and parsley in a bowl.
- Mix honey, olive oil and grapefruit juice and pour over salad.
- Mix well.
- Serve.

Pasta with Broad Beans and Smoked Salmon

Serves 2

Ingredients
2 cups pasta (les pâtes)
1 tbsp olive oil (l'huile d'olive)
1 clove garlic (l'ail), crushed
3 slices smoked salmon (le saumon fume), chopped
2 cups broad breans (les féves), cooked
80ml cream (la crème)
Handful of mint (le menthe), finely chopped
Fresh parmesan, grated

Instructions
- Cook pasta.
- Heat oil in a large pan, add garlic, salmon and broad beans and cook over a gentle heat until garlic and salmon are cooked.
- Add mint and cream.
- Stir.
- Serve with freshly grated parmesan.

Pasta with Clams

Serves 2

Ingredients
400g clams (la palourde)
2 cups pasta (les pâtes)
2 tbsps olive oil (l'huile d'olive)
2 cloves garlic (l'ail), thinly sliced
1 red chilli (le piment rouge), finely chopped
1 cup dry white wine (le vin blanc)
1 handful fresh parlsey (le persil), chopped
zest ¼ lemon (le citron)

Instructions
- One by one throw clams into a large bowl to dislodge sand and throw away any that do not react as they will be dead.
- Put live clams into another bowl and cover with water. Do this several times to rinse sand out of the clams.
- Cook pasta.
- Heat oil, garlic and chilli.
- Add clams to garlic and chill and cook for 30 seconds.
- Add wine and half the parsley and cook over a medium heat for about 4 minutes, stirring from time to time. Discard any unopened clams.
- Stir in the pasta and serve with the remaining parsley and lemon zest.

Creamy Ham Pasta

Serves 2

Ingredients

2 cups pasta (les pâtes)
1 tbsp olive oil (l'huile d'olive)
1 clove garlic, finely chopped
100g ham (le jambon) preferably jambon de bayonne, chopped
2 tbsps lemon juice (le citron)
½ cup cream (la crème)
1 tbsp fresh parsley (le persil), finely chopped
Fresh parmesan, grated

Instructions

- Cook pasta.
- Fry garlic in butter over a gentle heat.
- Add pasta, ham, cream, parsley and lemon juice and heat through.
- Serve with freshly grated parmesan.

Pasta with Artichokes and Peas

Serves 2

Ingredients
2 cups pasta (les pâtes)
100g fresh peas in their pods (les petits pois), shelled
10 marinated artichokes (l'artichaut), roughly chopped
1 tbsp olive oil (l'huile d'olive)
1 small shallot (l'échalote), finely chopped
1 clove garlic (l'ail), finely chopped
zest and juice of ½ a lemon (le citron)
125ml dry white wine (le vin blanc)
1 tsp capers (la câpre), finely chopped
1 tbsp fresh parsley (le persil), finely chopped
parmesan to serve

Instructions
- Cook pasta.
- Gently cook shallot and garlic in oil until softened.
- Add artichokes, lemon juice and zest, wine and capers.
- Simmer and reduce the liquid.
- Add pasta and parsley.
- Serve with freshly grated parmesan.

Leek and Lardon Risotto

Serves 2

Ingredients
100g lardons
4 small leeks (le poireau), trimmed and finely sliced
2 cloves garlic (l'ail), crushed
½ cup arborio rice (le riz arborio)
1 cup white wine (le vin blanc)
½ litre vegetable stock (le bouillon de légumes)
2 tbsps grated parmesan

Instructions
- Heat lardons in a frying pan.
- Add leeks and garlic and cook until soft.
- Add rice and stir to coat rice in fat from the lardons.
- Regularly stir risotto and add wine and stock in small quantities for about 20 minutes or until rice is cooked.
- Stir in parmesan.
- Serve with more parmesan grated on top of risotto.

Scallop and Prawn Risotto

Serves 2

Ingredients

2tbsps olive oil (l'huile d'olive)
1 shallot (l'échalote), finely chopped
2 cloves garlic (l'ail), finely chopped
½ cup arborio rice (le riz arborio)
1 cup white wine (le vin blanc)
vegetable stock (le bouillon de légumes)
Scallops (la coquille Saint-Jacques), uncooked
Prawns (la crevette), uncooked
2 tbsps paremesan, grated
parsley (le persil)

Instructions

- Heat oil in a frying pan.
- Add shallots and gently cook until soft.
- Add garlic and rice and stir, coating rice with the oil.
- Regularly stir risotto and add wine and stock in small quantities for about 20 minutes or until rice is cooked.
- After 15 minutes add scallops and prawns.
- Stir in parmesan when rice is almost cooked and scallops and prawns are fully cooked.
- Serve with more parmesan grated on top of risotto.

Asparagus and Lemon Risotto

Ingredients

1 bunch asparagus (l'asperges), cut into 2cm lengths
1 tbsp olive oil (l'huile d'olives)
1 tsp butter (le beure)
1 shallot (l'échalote), finely chopped
½ cup arborio rice (le riz arborio)
½ cup white wine (le vin blanc)
500ml vegetable stock (le bouillon de légumes)
Zest and juice of ½ a lemon (le citron)
2 tbsps paremesan, grated

Instructions

- Cook asparagus, refresh under cold water and set aside.
- Heat oil and butter in a frying pan.
- Add shallots and gently cook until soft.
- Add rice and stir, coating rice with oil and butter.
- Regularly stir risotto and add wine and stock in small quantities for about 20 minutes or until the rice is cooked.
- A few minutes before rice is cooked add asparagus, lemon zest and juice and parmesan.
- Stir well and serve with grated parmesan.

FISH/SHELLFISH

Types of Fish

OILY FISH - herring (l'hareng), mackerel (le maquereau), salmon (le saumon), trout (la truite), whitebait (la blanchaille), eel (l'anguille).

> These fish suit barbecuing and frying. Try dusting with a little flour and frying in a little butter and oil along with some chopped garlic.

MEDITERRANEAN FISH (neither oily nor non oily) - bream (la brème), gurnard (le rouget grondin), mullet (le rouget), sea bass (le bar).

> Ideally cook on a barbecue or with Mediterranean ingredients like olive oil, garlic, aromatic herbs, olives and anchovies.

ROUND FISH (non oily) - Cod family -cod (cabillaud), haddock (l'aiglefin), hake (le colin, le merlu), ling (le lingue julienne), Pollack (le lieu jeune), whiting (le merlan), monkfish (la lotte de mer), john dory (le saint-pierre).

> These fish can be pan fried, stir fried, steamed and barbecued.

FLAT FISH (non oily) - brill (le barbue), halibut (le flétan), plaice (le carrelet), sole (la limande-sole), turbot (le turbot).

> These fish are best pan fried. Try pan frying with a little butter and oil, chopped tomato, crushed garlic, lemon juice and some fresh chopped basil.

LARGE FISH (non oily) - Skate (la raie), shark (le requin), swordfish (le poisson-épée / l'espadron), tuna (le thon), conger eel (le congre).

> Try barbecuing steaks, making kebabs or pan frying. Marinade beforehand in olive oil, lemon juice and fresh thyme.

Mediterranean Fish

Serves 2

Ingredients
2 fish fillets - Either bream (la brême), gurnard (le rouget grondin), mullet (le rouget) or sea bass (le bar)
2 tbsps olive oil (l'huile d'olive)
2 cloves garlic (l'ail), finely sliced
500g cherry tomatoes (la tomate cerise) halved
2 tbsps balsamic vinegar (le vinaigre balsamique)
Handful green olives (l'olive), sliced
Handful basil (le basillic), chopped

Instructions
- Heat oil in frying pan and add fish fillets, skin down.
- Add garlic, tomatoes, balsamic vinegar and olives.
- When fish is cooked add basil and stir.
- Serve.

Creamy Monkfish

Serves 2

Ingredients

1 tbsp butter (le beurre)

1 small shallot (l'échalote), finely chopped

150g Monkfish (la lotte de mer), cut into chunks

2 slices smoked salmon (le saumon), chopped

150g baby mushrooms (le champignon), halved

100g Prawns (la crevette), raw

Juice ½ lemon (le citron)

80ml dry white wine (le vin blanc)

125 ml vegetable stock (le bouillon de légumes)

40ml cream (la crème)

Instructions

- Sweat shallots until opaque.
- Add mushrooms, monkfish, smoked salmon, prawns and lemon juice and cook.
- Once cooked remove mushrooms, monkfish, smoked salmon and prawns and keep warm.
- Add wine, vegetable stock and cream. Reduce to half.
- Add mushrooms, monkfish, smoked salmon and prawns. Heat through.
- Serve with potatoes and salad or fresh bread and salad.

Sea Bass with Lemon and Capers

Serves 2

Ingredients

4 fillets Sea bass (le bar)
1 tbsp olive oil (l'huile d'olive)
1 tbsp Butter (le beurre)
Juice of ½ lemon (le citron)
2 tbsps capers (la câpre)
Handful parsley (le persil), chopped

Instructions

- Cook sea bass skin down in hot oil.
- Once cooked add butter, lemon juice and capers.
- Heat gently for a minute.
- Add parsley and stir.
- Serve with potatoes or bread and vegetables or salad.

Sea Bass with Fennel and Wine

Serves 2

Ingredients

4 fillets Sea Bass (le bar)

1 bulb fennel (le feneuil), finely sliced

1 tbsp butter (le beurre)

1 cup white wine (le vin blanc)

Instructions

- Cook fennel in wine until the wine has reduced.
- Add butter and sea bass on top of fennel, skin side down and cook sea bass.
- Add water or extra wine if the fennel is becoming too dry before the fish has cooked.
- Serve sea bass on a bed of fennel with potatoes and vegetables.

Mussels with Leeks and Cider

Serves 2

Ingredients
1 kg fresh mussels (la moule)
1 tbsp olive oil (l'huile d'olive)
2 shallots (l'échalote), finely chopped
1 leek (le poireau), finely chopped
1 clove garlic (l'ail), finely chopped
250ml farm cider (le cidre)
1 tbsp crème fraiche
handful of fresh parsley (le persil), finely chopped

Instructions
- Wash mussels under cold running water removing any beards and discarding broken or dead mussels.
- Gently cook shallots and leeks in a large pan with olive oil until softened.
- Add garlic and cook for 1 minute and then add cider.
- Add mussels, cover and cook for 3-4 minutes until all mussels have opened. Discard any that haven't opened.
- Stir in Crème fraiche, parsley and seasoning.
- Serve with fresh bread.

Whiting with Tomato, Thyme and Pinenuts

Serves 2

Ingredients
4 fillets whiting (le merlan)
Flour (la farine)
250g cherry tomatoes (la tomate cerise), halved
2 tbsp toasted pine nuts (le pignon de pin)
1 tsp fresh thyme (le thym)
2 tbsps olive oil (l'huile d'olive)
Juice 1 lemon (le citron)
Salt and pepper (le sel et le poivre)

Instructions
- Dust skin side of fish in flour.
- Gently heat olive oil in a frying pan and add whiting skin side down.
- Add tomatoes, pine nuts, thyme, lemon juice and season with salt and pepper.
- Once whiting is cooked remove from frying pan and place on plates and spoon over the tomato sauce.
- Serve with Fresh bread or potatoes and a salad.

MEAT

Simple Ideas for Cooking Meat

Lamb or Chicken with Thyme and Garlic
4 lamb cutlets (côtelette d'agneau) or 2 chicken fillets (le poulet) •
1 tbsp fresh thyme (le thym), chopped • 2 tbsps olive oil (huile
d'olive) • 8 cloves garlic (l'ail) • 4 tbsps butter (le beurre) • Salt and
pepper (sel et poivre)

- Rub thyme into meat.
- Heat oil and 2 tbsps butter in a frying pan. Once very hot,
  add meat and cook quickly until brown on both sides.
- Lower the heat.
- Season meat and add remaining butter. When it begins to
  sizzle add garlic and cook until soft and brown.
- Place meat on plates and pour over the juices.

Beef - Peppered Steak
2 fillet steaks (le filet de boef) • 2 tbsps butter (le beurre) • 1 clove
garlic (l'ail), crushed • 1 tbsp Calvados • 2 tbsps cream (la crème)

- Press pepper and garlic into steaks.
- Heat butter in frying pan. Add steak to frying pan and cook
  as desired.
- Remove steak and keep warm.
- Add calvados and cream to pan and heat.
- Put steaks onto plates and pour over sauce.

Beef Fillet with Crème Fraiche

Serves 2

Ingredients

2 fillets of beef (le filet de boeuf)
60ml Pineau des Charantes
½ cup crème fraiche (la crème fraiche)
1 tbsp olive oil (l'huile d'olive)

Instructions

- Marinade beef in Pineau des Charantes for 30 minutes.
- Fry beef on both sides in oil over a medium heat.
- Remove beef and set aside.
- Add marinade to frying pan juices and cook over a medium heat for a few minutes.
- Add crème fraiche, stir and pour over beef.
- Serve with potatoes and vegetables.

Chicken with Cream and Mushrooms

Serves 2

Ingredients

1 tbsp olive oil (l'huile d'olive)
2 chicken breasts (le poulet)
150 g mushrooms (le champignon), quartered
250 ml vegetable stock (le bouillon de légumes)
1 tbsp Calvados
125 ml cream (la crème)
juice ½ lemon (le citron)
salt and pepper (le sel et le poivre)

Instructions

- Heat oil in a frying pan and cook chicken over a moderate heat for about 10-15 minutes.
- Add mushrooms and fry for 5 minutes, stirring occasionally.
- Add stock.
- Simmer gently for about 20 minutes or until chicken is completely cooked.
- Remove chicken, cover and keep warm.
- Add Calvados to the frying pan and bring to the boil and boil for 2 minutes.
- Add cream and lemon juice, and boil until the liquid is thickened.
- Season and return chicken to the frying pan and heat for about 5 minutes.
- Serve with fresh bread and salad or potatoes and vegetables.

Chicken Provençal

Serves 2

Ingredients

2 chicken breasts (le poulet)
1 tbsp olive oil (l'huile d'olive)
1 small onion (l'oignon), finely chopped
3 cloves garlic (l'ail), crushed
1tsp sugar (le sucre)
250 ml rosé wine (le vin rosé)
250g tomatoes (la tomate)

Instructions

- Put tomatoes in boiling water for 2 minutes. Remove from water. Peel and halve.
- Heat oil in frying pan and add chicken and cook for 10 minutes.
- Add onions and sauté for 1 -2 minutes until soft.
- Add garlic and cook for 1 minute.
- Add sugar, tomatoes and wine. Cook for 10 minutes or until tomatoes have softened and wine has reduced.
- Make sure chicken is thoroughly cooked.
- Serve with new potatoes or bread and salad.

Pork with Apples and Calvados

Serves 2

Ingredients

2 Pork fillets (le filet de porc) thinly sliced
2 tbsps. butter (le beurre)
1 apple (la pomme), finely sliced
1 tsp sugar (le sucre)
1 large shallot (l'échalote), chopped
1tbsp chopped fresh thyme (le thym), chopped
¼ cup Calvados
¼ cup cider (le cidre)
200 ml carton of cream (la crème)

Instructions

- Melt 1 tbsp butter in a pan over medium heat.
- Add apples and sugar to the pan and gently cook until golden brown, set aside.
- Melt 1 tbsp butter in frying pan over high heat and add pork and sauté until cooked.
- Add shallots and thyme and sauté 2 minutes.
- Add Calvados and boil until reduced to glaze. Remove pork and set aside. Stir in cream and cider, boil until mixture thickens.
- Season and add pork and warm through.
- Arrange pork on plates. Spoon over sauce. Arrange apple slices alongside pork.
- Serve with fresh bread and salad or potatoes and vegetables.

ONE POT MEALS

Omelettes

Serves 2

Ingredients
3 eggs (l'oeuf), beaten
1 tbsp butter (le beurre)
2 tbsps oil (l'huile d'olive)
salt and pepper (le sel et le poivre)

Instructions
- Heat butter and oil in a frying pan over a high heat.
- When butter and oil begin to foam add eggs.
- Add additional ingredients and cook until egg is cooked.
- Serve.

Suggested fillings
Asparagus (l'asperges) and ham (le jambon)
Grated cheese (le fromage)
Courgettes (la courgette), capers (la câpre) and anchovies
        (l'anchois)
Mushrooms (le champignon) and a little grated truffle (la truffe)
Cooked onions (l'oignon)
Herbs (les herbes)
Tomatoes (la tomate)
Spinach (l'épinard) or swiss chard (la blette)
Leeks (le poireau)
Chopped olives (l'olive)
Artichoke hearts (Coeur d'artichaut)
Red pepper (le poivron rouge),ham (jambon de bayonne),
        tomatoes (la tomate), parsley (le persil) and garlic (l'ail)

Galettes

Galettes are savoury pancakes made with buckwheat flour and are different to sweet pancakes (les crèpes). They are made up with savoury fillings. The easiest way to make galettes is to buy precooked ones. Choose the best you can find. These only take a couple of minutes to heat in a frying pan.

- Prepare fillings before heating galettes.
- Heat a nob of butter in a frying pan.
- Place galette in frying pan and put filling in galette.
- Heat for a couple of minutes.
- Serve.

Suggested Fillings
Grated cheese (le fromage).
Coarsely chopped onion (l'oignon) sautéed in butter (le beure).
Sliced mushrooms (le champignon) sautéed in butter (le beure) and
      crushed garlic (l'ail).
Lardons (100 g) with 2 finely chopped tomatoes (la tomate), 1
      onion (l'oignon) cooked slowly with butter (le beure) and a
      little cider (le cidre).
Smoked salmon and crème fraiche.
Sliced ham and grated cheese.

Vegetable Soup

Serves 2

Ingredients

1 small onion (l'oignon), chopped
1 clove garlic (l'ail), crushed
1 carrot (la carotte), sliced
2 celery sticks (le céleri-en-branche), sliced
1 leek (le poireau), sliced
1 tbsp unsalted butter (le beurre doux)
1 courgette (la courgette), sliced
2 tomatoes (la tomate), peeled and chopped
500 ml water (l'eau), boiling
 salt and pepper (le sel et le poivre)

Instructions

- In a saucepan gently heat onion, garlic, carrot, celery and leeks in butter for 5 minutes over a medium heat.
- Season.
- Add courgette, tomato and boiling water.
- Boil for 5-7 minutes over a high heat until vegetables are just tender.

Vegetable Soup with Chorizo

Serves 2

Ingredients

1 tbsp olive oil (l'huile d'olive)

1 onion (l'oignon), chopped

1 clove garlic (l'ail), crushed

4 tomatoes (la tomate), peeled and finely chopped

1 carrot (la carotte), finely chopped

2 sticks celery (le céleri-en-branche), sliced

500 ml vegetable stock (le bouillon de légumes)

approximately 2 inches of chorizo sausage, thinly sliced

Instructions

- Heat oil in pan and sauté onion for 1 minute.
- Add garlic, tomatoes, carrot, celery, vegetable stock and chorizo and cook over moderate heat for 20 minutes or until the vegetables are cooked.
- Serve with fresh bread.

Clam and Vegetable Soup

Serves 2

Ingredients

2 tbsps olive oil (l'huile d'olive)

2 cloves garlic (l'ail), crushed

1 small red chilli (le piment), seeded and chopped

1 small leek (le poireau), sliced

1 small onion (l'oignon), sliced

1 carrot (la carotte), finely sliced

1 red pepper (le poivron rouge), finely sliced

500 ml water (l'eau)

24 small clams (la palourde), well rinsed

1 small bunch of fresh parsley (le persil), chopped

Instructions

- Sweat garlic, chilli, leek, onion, carrot and red pepper in oil for 3 minutes. Pour in water and simmer for 10 minutes.
- Add clams and boil as quickly as possible until they open. Discard any that do not open.
- Pour into bowls and sprinkle with parsley.
- Serve with fresh bread.

DESSERTS

Chocolate Fondue

Serves 2

Ingredients

100g milk chocolate (le chocolat), broken into pieces
60 ml cream (la crème)

Fruit - any of the following:
Strawberries (la fraise)
Kiwi fruit (le kiwi), sliced
Pear (la poire), sliced
Banana (la banana)

Instructions

- Place chocolate in a saucepan and gently melt over a low heat.
- Stir occasionally, until smooth.
- Add cream and warm through.
- Remove from heat.
- Pour into a serving bowl and serve with fruit.

Bananas with Chocolate

Serves 2

Ingredients
1 tbsp butter (le beurre)
1 tbsp sugar (le sucre)
2 bananas (la banane), peeled and sliced diagonally
2 tbsps Pineau de Charantes
A small amount of 70% dark chocolate (le chocolat), grated
Crème fraiche

Instructions
- Melt butter in a frying pan over a medium heat.
- Stir in sugar and add bananas and cook until caramelised - around 3 minutes.
- Add the Pineau de Charantes and cook until evaporated - around 30 seconds.
- Sprinkle with chocolate and cook until melted.
- Serve with crème fraiche

Melon with Sweet Wine

Serves 2

Ingredients

1 cavallion or galia melon (le melon)

sweet white wine (le vin blanc) like a Sauternes

Instructions

- Cut melon in half and remove the seeds.
- Pour in a generous amount of chilled wine and serve.

Chestnuts in Wine

Serves 2

Ingredients

200 g chestnuts (la châtaigne / le marron)
1 x 5 cm long ribbon orange zest (l'orange)
200 ml Sauternes wine (le vin)
 75 ml red wine (le vin rouge)
2 tbsps sugar (le sucre)
crème fraiche or fromage frais to serve

Instructions

- Put chestnuts, orange zest, Sauternes, red wine and sugar in pan.
- Bring to the boil and simmer gently until wine has reduced to a thick syrup – approximately 30 minutes.
- Put into bowls and serve with crème fraiche or fromage frais.

Crèpes

Ingredients
3 eggs (l'oeuf)
1 cup flour (la farine de blé)
500 ml milk (le lait)
butter (le beurre) for frying

Makes approximately 12 small crèpes

Instructions
- Mix flour and eggs and add milk slowly to avoid lumps.
- Rest for ½ hour.
- Melt 1 tbsp butter in frying pan and mix melted butter into mixture.
- Pour just enough crèpe mixture into frying pan and cook on both sides.
- Add filling and serve.
- Do the same for the rest of the crèpes.

Suggested Fillings for Crèpes
Beurre sucre – a little melted butter sprinkled with sugar.
Crème de maron.
Butter sprinkled with powdered drinking chocolate.
Caramel.
Apples – serves 2 - 1 apple (la pomme), 1 tbsp demerara sugar (le sucre brun), 1 tbsp butter (le beurre), 1 tbsp Calvados.
Oranges – Serves 2 – peel two oranges and slice between thin membranes to remove segments. Put into pan with 2 tbsps sugar (sucre) and 2 tbsps Cointreau - Heat until sugar has dissolved and liquid has become syrupy.

Fruit Salad

Serves 2

Ingredients
½ cup sugar (le sucre)
½ cup water (l'eau)
100 ml red wine (le vin rouge)
1 peach (la pêche), sliced
1 apricot (l'abricot), sliced
½ orange peel (l'orange)
60 g raspberries (la framboise)
60 g red current (la groseille)
60 g cherries (la cerise)
1 tbsp calvados

Instructions
- Mix sugar, water and wine in saucepan and heat until syrupy. Leave to cool.
- Prepare fruit and put into bowls.
- Pour over syrup and calvados.
- Serve with fromage frais.

Peaches in Calvados

Serves 2

Ingredients
⅓ cup Calvados
1 tbsp sugar (le sucre)
2 peaches (la pêche)
Fromage frais to serve

Instructions
- Put peaches in boiling water for a couple of minutes to loosen the skins.
- Peel peaches and remove stone and cut into quarters.
- Place peaches, Calvados and sugar in a bowl.
- Leave for a couple of hours in a fridge.
- Serve with fromage frais.

Poached Peaches and Apricots

Serves 2

Ingredients
2 tbsps sugar (le sucre)
360 ml dry white wine (le vin blanc sec)
2 strawberries (la fraise)
4 peaches (la pêche), peeled
4 apricots (l'abricot), peeled
fromage frais to serve

Instructions
- Put sugar and wine in a saucepan and heat gently until sugar has dissolved.
- Bring to the boil and cook for 3 - 4 minutes.
- Add fruit and boil for 6 - 7 minutes or until peaches are soft.
- Remove fruit and boil until liquid has become a syrup.
- Put into bowls and serve with fromage frais.

Cooks notes
To peel peaches and apricots, put whole fruit into a bowl of boiling water. Leave for 1 - 2 minutes then drain. The skins should then peel away easily. If fruit is not quite ripe simmer gently in a little sugar and water solution for about 6 - 8 minutes or until just tender. Drain and peel.

MISCELLANEOUS

Suggested Store Cupboard Essentials

To take

- Capers
- Extra virgin olive oil
- Balsamic vinegar
- Mustard
- Flour
- Sugar
- Sea salt
- Pine nuts
- Vegetable stock cubes
- Pepper mill
- Garlic
- Honey
- Risotto Rice
- Pasta
- Couscous
- Quinoa

Growing Herbs:

Parsley / Basil / Mint / Thyme

It is difficult to buy growing herbs in French supermarkets. Parsley is the most used herb in this book so if you are only going to take one herb take parsley.

Utensils to take:

- Measuring spoons and measuring cups
- Whisk (for pancakes)
- Potato peeler

- Grater
- Garlic crusher
- Spatula
- Sharp Knife
- Frying pan and sauce pan
- Cutlery
- Plates and bowls
- Plastic storage pots
- Aluminium foil
- Plastic food bags
- Kitchen roll
- Thermos
- Gas stove

You could also bring:
- Tinned artichokes
- Tinned anchovies
- Bottled green olives

Measurements

¼ cup of rice per person
1 cup of pasta per person
¼ cup of couscous per person
¼ cup of quinoa per person

1 ml - millilitre
1 cl - centilitre = 10 ml
1 dl - décalitre = 100 ml
1 lt - litre = 1000 ml

Cs - c à soupe - cuiller à soupe = tablespoon - tbsp
Cc - c à café - cuiller à café = teaspoon - tsp

60ml = ¼ cup
80ml = ⅓ cup
125ml = ½ cup
250ml = 1 cup

Picnics

In addition to sandwiches and salads here are some picnic ideas which can be sourced either from the market and local shops:

From the epicerie:
- Breadsticks
- Juice cartons and bottles of water
- Crisps
- Rotiserie chicken

From the charcuterie:
- Patés
- sliced cured sausages

From the fromagerie:
- Local cheeses

From the boulangerie:
- Baguette
- Fougas bread

From the marché:
- Olives
- artichoke hearts
- sundried tomatoes
- tapenade
- Baby tomatoes
- Fruit including: bananas, apples, apricots, strawberries, pears, plums, peaches etc

Sandwiches

Sandwich Ideas

Here are some ideas for sandwiches. Some obvious but easily forgotten and other ones to tempt the tastebuds:

Cheese and Tomato / Smoked Salmon and Cream Cheese / Tomato / Ham and Cheese / Cucumber / Radish / Egg and Cress / Egg and Rocket / Avocado and Prawn Mayonnaise / Avocado, Rocket and Lime Mayonnaise

Tuna Baguette
1 baguette
1 tin tuna (le thon), drained
1 tbsp capers (la câpre)
Handful rocket (la rocquette)
2 tbsps mayonnaise (la mayonnaise)

Baguette with Asparagus and Jambon de Bayonne
1 baguette
8 spears of asparagus (l'asperges), cooked
8 slices of Jambon de Bayonne

Baguette with Aubergine, Jambon de Bayonne and Olives
1 baguette
1 aubergine (l'aubergine), fried in olive oil
8 slices jambon de Bayonne
8 large green olives (l'olives), finely sliced

Barbecue

Marinades

Honey and Lemon Marinade for Beef
1 tsp honey
2 tbsps lemon juice
2 cloves garlic, crushed

Pineau de Charantes Marinade
2 tbsps Pineau de Charantes
1 tbsp honey
1 clove garlic, crushed

Salsa
4 tomatoes (la tomate), finely chopped
1 small red onion (l'oignon rouge), finely chopped
1 clove garlic (l'ail), crushed
½ red chilli (le piment rouge) finely chopped
Juice of 1 lime (le citron vert)
1 tbsp olive oil (l'huile d'olive)

Olive and Cucumber Relish
20ml olive oil
50g pitted green olives (l'olive), chopped
Juice 1 lemon (le citron)
¼ cucumber (le concombre), peeled, seeded and diced
1 small chilli (le piment rouge), finely chopped
Handful parsley (le persil), chopped

Food Pairings

Here is a basic list of foods that work well together.

Anchovy - capers, lemon.

Artichokes - olive oil, lemon, thyme, garlic.

Aubergines - olive oil, garlic, courgettes.

Avocados - lime, chilli.

Beetroot - watercress, walnuts, orange.

Celery - apple, blue cheese, chestnuts.

Courgettes - garlic, olive oil, herbs, tomatoes.

Cucumber - mint, yoghurt.

Fennel - pork, olives.

Figs - cured ham like jambon de Bayonne.

Goats cheese - smoked salmon, capers.

Mushrooms - chestnuts, truffles.

Peaches - mango.

Peppers - basil, olive oil, tomatoes, anchovies, garlic.

Tomatoes - basil, garlic, avocado.

Strawberry - peaches.

APPENDIX

Fruit and Vegetables - les fruits et les legumes

l'abricot – apricot

l'ail – garlic

l'ananas – pineapple

l'artichaut - artichoke

Using sharp knife cut off stork leaving the base flat, remove outer leaves. Trim outside of artichoke, cut off top and remove choke. Rub with lemon to prevent it going black. **To cook**: Boil in pan until petals part easily from globe. Serve with garlic butter.

l'asperges – asparagus

Cook in boiling water until soft and serve with garlic butter.

l'aubergine - aubergine (eggplant)

Aubergines may be purple or white and vary in size.

l'avocat - avocado

Cut avocado in half, remove stone and serve with small amount of balsamic vinegar.

la banane – banana

la betterave rouge – beetroot

la blette - swiss chard

le broccoli – broccoli

la carotte – carrot

le cassis – black currant

la cébette - spring onion

le céleri-en-branche – celery

le céleri-rave – celeriac

To cook: Peel like a potato, rinse and sprinkle with lemon juice. Cut into pieces and cook in boiling water for 5 minutes. Can be served as a boiled vegetable.

le cèpe – ceps or boletus mushroom

la cerise - cherry

le champignon – mushroom

la châtaigne – chestnut

A small edible chestnut with two or three kernels in each husk. See also le marron.

le chou – cabbage

le chou-fleur – cauliflower

le chou frisé de Milan - savoy cabbage

Remove withered outer leaves. Cut cabbage into quarters and cook for around 12 minutes in boiling lightly salted water. Drain and cool. Cut into matchsticks. Pour over with dressing [2 tbsps olive oil (l'huile d'olive), 1 tbsp lemon juice (le citron)] and sprinkle with chopped spring onions.

Le chou-rave - kholrabi

le citron – lemon

le citron vert – lime

le concombre – cucumber

le cornichon - gherkin

le cou de Bruxelles - Brussel sprout

la courge - squash

la courgette - courgette (zucchini)

le cresson - watercress

l'échalote – shallot

l'endive – chicory

Can be served with a mustard dressing sprinkled with hazelnuts

les épinards – spinach

le fenouil - fennel

les féves - broad beans

la figue – fig

la fraise – strawberry

la framboise – raspberry

la grenade – pomegranate

la groseille - red currant

These can be eaten raw sprinkled with sugar or in a fruit salad.

le haricot vert - green bean / French bean

la mâche - lambs lettuce

la laiture – lettuce

le marron – chestnut

le melon – melon

la mirabelle - mirabelle plum

    These are best eaten stewed.

la morille – morel mushroom

la mûre - blackberry

le navet – turnip

l'olive - olive

l'oignon – onion

l'orange – orange

l'oseille - sorrel

le pamplemousse – grapefruit

la pêche - peach

les petits pois – peas

le piment – chilli pepper

la pleurotte – oyster mushroom

la poire - pear

le poireau – leek

le poivron – pepper, capsicum

la pomme - apple

la pomme de terre - potato

le potimarron - potimarron squash

    A small pumpkin or gourd which has a slight chestnuty taste.

le potiron - pumpkinl

la prune - plum

le radis - radish

le radis noir - black radish

    Peel, slice finely and put on buttered bread.

le radis blanc - daikon radish or mooli

le rasin - grape

la reine-claude - greengage

    A type of plum that is delicious eaten fresh.

la rhubarb - rhubarb

la rocquette - rocket

la scarole - escarole (batavia)

    Eaten raw in a salad. As a winter salad, serve with nuts and raisins.

la tomate - tomato

la tomate cerise - cherry tomato

la tomate sechée - sundried tomato

le topinambour- jerusalem artichoke

la truffe - truffle

Fish and Shellfish - les Poissons et les Fruits de Mer

l'anchois – anchovy

l'aiglefin - haddock

le congre - conger eel

l'anguille de roche – conger eel

l' anguille de sable – sand eel

    These can be dug out of the sand at low tide and cooked like whitebait (la blanchaille)

le bar - sea bass

    Can be cooked on a barbecue. Alternatively cook with olive oil, garlic, thyme, olives and anchovies.

la barbue - brill

    Similar to turbot

le bigorneau - winkle

    Can be found on the shoreline at low tide. Wash in cold water, bring to the boil in salted water and boil for 2 mins. Drain and eat with shallot sauce.

la blanchaille - whitebait

    These should be no bigger than 5-6cm long. Wash thoroughly, dust in flour and deep fry.

la brème - bream

    Can be cooked on a barbecue. Alternatively cook with olive oil, garlic, thyme, olives and anchovies.

le brochet - pike

le cabillaud – cod

le carrelet - plaice

le colin – hake

la coquille Saint-Jacques – scallop

le crabe – crab

la crevette – prawn

> Serve cooked with mayonnaise.

la daurade - gilt head bream

> This is the best tasting bream and can be cooked on a barbecue.

l'écrevisse – crayfish

> A fresh water crustacean which looks like a small lobster. Cook as you would a lobster or langoustine.

l'églefin - haddock

l'encornet - squid

l'espadon - swordfish

le flétan - halibut

l'hareng - herring

l'homard – lobster

> Serve cooked with mayonnaise.

l'huître – oyster

> Traditionally oysters are eaten raw with buttered bread and a squeeze of lemon juice or a drop of vinegar. You will need a special tool for opening the oysters and most large French supermarkets will sell these.

le lançon - sand eel

> These can be dug out of the sand at low tide and should be cooked like whitebait (la blanchaille)

la langoustine - langoustine - Dublin Bay prawn

> Serve cooked with mayonnaise.

le lieu jeune – pollack

> Related to whiting. Cook as you would cod or whiting.

la limande-sole - lemon sole

> Can be cooked like Dover sole or with a little butter and freshly ground salt and pepper.

le lingue julienne – ling

Similar to monkfish (la lotte de mer).

la lotte de mer – monkfish

Can also be barbecued.

le maquereau - mackerel

le merlan – whiting

le merlu - hake

la merluche – dried cod

le merou – grouper

la morue – cod

la moule – mussel

l'orphie - garfish

la palourde – clam

le poisson-épée - swordfish

le poulpe - octopus

la raie - skate

The wings are usually only sold. Poach the wing in white wine vinegar (le vinaigre vin blanc). Add thyme (le thym) and pepper (le poivre) and cook for 6 – 8 minutes. Serve with a salad.

le requin - shark

le rouget - mullet

Can be cooked on a barbecue. Alternatively cook with olive oil, garlic, thyme, olives and anchovies.

le rouget barbet - red mullet

Can be cooked on a barbecue. Alternatively cook with olive oil, garlic, thyme, olives and anchovies.

le rouget de vase - striped mullet

Can be cooked on a barbecue. Alternatively cook with olive oil, garlic, thyme, olives and anchovies.

le rouget grondin - gurnard

Can be cooked on a barbecue. Alternatively cook with olive oil, garlic, thyme, olives and anchovies.

le saint-pierre - john dory

Can be barbecued or cooked like any flat fish.

le saumon – salmon

Can also be cooked on a barbecue.

la sardine – sardine

la seiche – cuttlefish

la sole - dover sole

le thon - tuna

le thon rouge - blue fin tuna

le tourteau = le crabe - crab

la truite - trout

le turbot - turbot

Serve with hollandaise sauce which can be bought in French supermarkets.

Meat - La Viande

l'agneau – lamb

le boeuf - beef

le cheval – horse

le chevreuil - venison

le porc - pork

le taureau - bull

le veau – veal

Cuts of Meat

French meat is cut differently to the meat in the UK.

l'aloyau – sirloin

la bavette – undercut beef steak comes from the skirt

bifteck/ steak – steak

la cervelle – brains

le collet - scrag (end) of lamb

la côtelette – lamb chop / lamb cutlet

Usually from the rack of lamb.

les côtes – loin chops

Rack of pork or chump of lamb.

le cou – neck

le cul – tail

l'echine – shoulder of pork or lamb

l'entrecôte – ribeye

le filet de porc - pork fillet

From the hind loin area of the pig. The English fillet is from the part the French know as jambon.

le filet de boef - beef fillet

le foie – liver

le gigot d'agneau - leg of lamb

le gigot de chevreuil - haunch of venison

le gîte (à la noix) - topside of beef

le grenadin de veau - veal medallion

le lardon – diced bacon

le jambon - ham

le jarret - lamb shank or shin

les joues – cheeks

la langue de bœuf - beef tongue

l'os - bone

l'os à moelle - marrowbone

le rognon - kidney

la poitrine – pork belly – bacon

la poitrine/ le poitrail – breast of lamb

le romsteak/ le rumsteak - rump steak

le saucisson - sausage (dried)

la saucisse - sausage (fresh or cooked)

la selle d'agneau – saddle of lamb

le steak à hacher- steak for mincing

Used for steak tartare or steak haché which looks like a burger.

la tête de veau - rolled veal head, including the tongue

le tournedos/ filet mignon – tenderloin beef or lamb steak
la tranche grasse – silverside of beef
la tranche – slice

Of a steak of any meat other than beef.

le travers de porc - spare rib of pork
viande avec l'os - meat on the bone

Poultry - La Volaille

le canard – duck
le canette, la cane - duck (female)
le chapon – capon
le coq - cockerel
le coquelet - cock (under 2lb)
le dinde – turkey
le pigeonneau – squab
la pintade - guinea hen
la poule – hen
le poulet - hen (young)
le poulet - chicken

(a young chicken of around 42 days old at the time of slaughter – normal age to buy a chicken for eating). Markets and supermarkets sell roast chicken which are great for picnics.

le poussin – chick

Cuts of Poultry

les cuisses – thighs
magret – breast

Game - Le Gibier

la bécasse – woodcock
la caille - quail
la faisan – pheasant
le lapin – rabbit
le lapereau - rabbit (young)
le lièvre – hare
le padre - partridge
le sanglier – wild boar

Grains - Les Céréales

le boulgour - bulgar wheat
le couscous – couscous
l'épeautre – spelt
les haricots oeil de perdrix - black eyed peas
les lentilles – lentils
le mais – sweetcorn
les pois chiches - chick peas
le quinoa - quinoa
le riz - rice

Herbs and Spices - les Herbes et les Épices

l' aneth - dill
le basilic – basil
la cannelle – cinnamon
la cardamome – cardamom
le cerfeuil – chervil
la ciboulette – chives
le clou de girofle – clove
l'estragon – tarragon

le feneuil – fennel

le gingembre - ginger

l'hysope – hyssop

le laurier – bay (la feuille de laurier – bay leaf)

la lavande – lavender

la marjolaine – marjoram

la menthe – mint

l'origan – oregano

le paprika – paprika

le persil – parsley

le poivre – pepper

la réglisse – liquorice

le romarin – rosemary

la sarriette – savory

la sauge – sage

le serpolet - wild thyme

le thym – thyme

le tilleul - lime blossom (linden)

la verveine – verbena

Dairy – la Crémerie

le beurre – butter

le beurre sale – salted butter

le beurre demi-sel – lightly salted butter

le beurre doux – unsalted butter

la crème – cream

le fromage – cheese

la glace - ice cream

le lait – milk

le lait écrémé – skimmed milk

le lait entire – full fat milk

le yaourt – yoghurt

le yaourt à la Grecque nature - Greek yoghurt

Nuts – Les Noix

la amande – almond
la cacahuète – peanut
la châtaigne – small edible chestnut
le marron – large edible chestnut
la noisette – hazelnut
la noix – walnut
la noix du Brésil - Brazil nut
la noix de coco - coconut
la noix de cajou - cashew nut
la pacane – pecan
le pignon de pin – pine nut (pine kernel)
la pistache –pistachio

Miscellaneous Produce

le bouillon – stock cube
le bouillon de volaille - chicken stock
la câpre – caper
la confiture – jam
la farine – flour
la farine d'avoine – oatmeal flour
la farine de blé – wheat flour
la farine de châtaigne – chestnut flour
la farine de froment – wheat flour
la farine de maïs – cornflour
la farine de sarrasin – buckwheat flour
la farine de seigle – rye flour
la farine de riz – rice flour
la glace pile – crushed ice
l'huile d'arachide – peanut oil
l'huile de colza – rapeseed oil

l'huile de noix – walnut oil

l'huile d'olive – olive oil

l'huile de séseme – seseme oil

l'huile de tournesol – sunflower oil

l'huile de végétale – vegetable oil

l'huile de première pression – vegetable oil from first pressing

l'huile de viege – extra virgin – olive oil from first cold pressing

la mayonnaise - mayonnaise

le miel – honey

le moutarde – mustard

les nouilles - noodles

le oeuf – egg

les pâtes – pasta

les pâtes alimentaires – dried pasta

les pâtes frâiches – fresh pasta

les pâtes à potage – soup noodles

le raisin sec – raisin

le sucre – sugar

le sucre cristallisé – granulated sugar

le sucre en poudre – caster sugar

le syrop de érable – maple syrup

le vinaigre – vinegar

le vinaigre vin blanc – white wine vinegar

le vinaigre vin rouge – red wine vinegar

le vinaigre balsamique – balsamic vinegar

A to Z - English to French

A
almond - la amande
anchovy - l'anchois
apple - la pomme
apricot - l'abricot
artichoke - l'artichaut
asparagus - l'asperges
aubergine (eggplant) - l'aubergine
avocado - l'avocat
B
bacon, diced - le lardon
banana - la banane
basil - le basilic
bay - le laurier
bay leaf - la feuille de laurier
beef - le bœuf
beef fillet - le filet de boeuf
beef tongue - la langue de bœuf
beef, topside of - le gîte (à la noix)
beetroot - la betterave rouge
black currant - le cassis
black eyed peas - les haricots oeil de perdrix
black radish - le radis noir
blackberry - la mûre
bone - l'os
brains - la cervelle
Brazil nut - la noix du Brésil
bream - la brème
breast - magret
brill - la barbue
broad beans - les féves
broccoli - le broccoli

Brussel sprout - le cou de Bruxelles

bulgar wheat - le boulgour

bull - le taureau

butter - le beurre

butter, lightly salted - le beurre demi-sel

butter, salted - le beurre sale

butter, unsalted - le beurre doux

C

cabbage - le chou

caper - la câpre

capon - le chapon

capsicum - le poivron

cardamom - la cardamome

carrot - la carotte

cashew nut - la noix de cajou

cauliflower - le chou-fleur

celeriac - le céleri-rave

celery - le céleri-en-branche

ceps or boletus mushroom - le cèpecherry - la cerise

cheeks - les joues

cheese - le fromage

cheese, goat - le fromage de chèvre

cheese, sheep - le fromage de brebis

cherry - la cerise

chestnut, large edible - le marron

chestnut, small edible - la châtaigne

chick - le poussin

chick peas - les pois chiches

chicken - le poulet

chicken stock - le bouillon de volaille

chicory - l'endive

chilli pepper - le piment

chives - la ciboulette

cinnamon - la cannelle

clam - la palourde

clove - le clou de girofle

cock (under 2lb) - le coquelet

cockerel - le coq

coconut - la noix de coco

cod, dried - la merluche

cod - la morue / le cabillaud

conger eel - le congre / l'anguille de roche

cornflour - la farine de maïs

courgette - la courgette

couscous - le couscous

crab - le crabe

crab - le tourteau / le crabe

crayfish - l'écrevisse

cream - la crème

cucumber - le concombre

cuttlefish - la seiche

D

daikon radish - le radis blanc

dill - l' aneth

Dover sole - la sole

Dublin Bay prawn - la langoustine

duck - le canard

duck (female) - le canette, la cane

E

egg - l'œuf

eggplant - l'aubergine

escarole (batavia) lettuce - la scarole

F

fennel - le feneuil

fig - la figue

flour - la farine

flour, buckwheat - la farine de sarrasin

flour, chestnut - la farine de châtaigne

flour, oatmeal - oatmeal la farine d'avoine
flour, rice - la farine de riz
flour, rye - la farine de seigle
flour, wheat - la farine de froment, la farine de blé
French bean - le haricot vert
G
garfish - l'orphie
garlic - l'ail
gherkin - le cornichon
gilt head bream - la daurade
ginger - le gingembre
grape - le rasin
grapefruit - le pamplemousse
Greek yoghurt - le yaourt à la Grecque nature
green bean - le haricot vert
greengage - la reine-claude
grouper - le merou
guinea hen - la pintade
gurnard - le rouget grondin
H
haddock - l'aiglefin / l'églefin
hake - le colin / le merlu
halibut - le flétan
ham - le jambon
hare - le lièvre
hazelnut - la noisette
hen - la poule
hen (young) - le poulet
herring - l'hareng
honey - le miel
horse - le cheval
hyssop - l'hysope
I
ice cream - la glace

ice, crushed - la glace pile

J

jam - la confiture

jerusalem artichoke - le topinambour

john dory - le saint-pierre

K

kholrabi - le chou-rave

kidney - le rognon

L

lamb - l'agneau

lamb chop / lamb cutlet - la côtelette

lamb shank or shin - le jarret

lamb, breast of - la poitrine/ le poitrail

lamb, leg of - le gigot d'agneau

lamb, saddle of - la selle d'agneau

lambs lettuce - la mâche

langoustine - la langoustine

lavender - la lavande

leek - le poireau

lemon - le citron

lemon sole - la limande-sole

lentils - les lentilles

lettuce - la laiture

lime - le citron vert

lime blossom (linden) - tilleul

ling - le lingue julienne

liquorice - la réglisse

liver - le foie

lobster - l'homard

loin chops - les côtes

M

mackerel - le maquereau

maple syrup - le syrop de érable

marjoram - la marjolaine

marrowbone - l'os à moelle

mayonnaise - la mayonnaise

meat on the bone - viande avec l'os

melon - le melon

milk - le lait

milk, full fat - le lait entire

milk, skimmed - le lait écrémé

mint - la menthe

mirabelle plum - la mirabelle

monkfish - la lotte de mer

mooli - le radis blanc

morel mushroom - la morille

mullet - le rouget

mushroom - le champignon

mussel - la moule

mustard - le moutarde

N

neck - le cou

noodles - les nouilles

noodles, soup - les pâtes à potage

O

octopus - le poulpe

olive - l'olive

olive oil - l'huile d'olive

olive oil, extra virgin - l'huile d'olive extra-viege

onion - l'oignon

orange - l'orange

oregano - l'origan

oyster - l'huître

oyster mushroom - la pleurotte

P

paprika - le paprika

parsley - le persil

partridge - le padre

pasta - les pâtes

pasta, dried - les pâtes alimentaires

pasta, fresh - les pâtes frâiches

peach - la pêche

peanut - la cacahuète

peanut oil - l'huile d'arachide

pear - la poire

peas - les petits pois

pecan - la pacane

pepper - le poivron

pepper - le poivre

pheasant - la faisan

pike - le brochet

pine nut / pine kernel - le pignon de pin

pineapple - l'ananas

pistachio - la pistache

plaice - le carrelet

plum - la prune

pollack - le lieu jeune

pomegranate - la grenade

pork - le porc

pork belly / bacon - la poitrine

pork fillet - le filet de porc

pork, spare rib of - le travers de porc

potato - la pomme de terre

potimarron squash - le potimarron

prawn - la crevette

pumpkin - le potiron

Q

quail - la caille

quinoa - le quinoa

R

rabbit - le lapin

rabbit (young) - le lapereau

radish - le radis

raisin - le raisin sec

rapeseed oil - l'huile de colza

raspberry - la framboise

red cabbage - le chou rouge

red currant - la groseille

red mullet - le rouget barbet

rhubarb - la rhubarbe

ribeye steak - l'entrecôte

rice - le riz

rocket - la rocquette

rosemary - le romarin

rump steak - le romsteak/ le rumsteak

S

sage - la sauge

salmon - le saumon

sand eel - l' anguille de sable / le lançon

sardine - la sardine

sausage, dried - le saucisson

sausage, fresh or cooked - la saucisse

savory - la sarriette

savoy cabbage - le chou frisé de Milan

scallop - la coquille Saint-Jacques

scrag (end) of lamb - le collet

sea bass - le bar

seseme oil - l'huile de séseme

shallot - l'échalote

shark - le requin

shoulder of pork or lamb - l'echine

silverside of beef - la tranche grasse

sirloin - l'aloyau

skate - la raie

slice - la tranche

sorrel - l'oseille

spelt - l'épeautre

spinach - les épinards

spring onion - la cébette

squab - le pigeonneau

squash - la courge

squid - l'encornet

steak - bifteck/ steak

steak for mincing - le steak à hacher

stock cube - le bouillon

strawberry - la fraise

striped mullet - le rouget de vase

sugar - le sucre

sugar, caster - le sucre en poudre

sugar, granulated - le sucre cristallisé

sunflower oil - l'huile de tournesol

sweetcorn - le maïs

swiss chard - la blette

swordfish - l'espadon

swordfish - le poisson-épée

T

tail - le cul

tarragon - l'estragon

tenderloin beef or lamb steak - le tournedos/ filet mignon

thighs - les cuisses

thyme - le thym

thyme, wild - le serpolet

tomato - la tomate

tomato, cherry - la tomate cerise

tomato puree - la purée de tomates

tomato, sundried - la tomate sechée

trout - la truite

truffle - la truffe

tuna - le thon

tuna, blue fin - le thon rouge

turbot - le turbot

turkey - le dinde

turnip - le navet

V

veal - le veau

veal head, rolled, including the tongue - la tête de veau

veal medallion - le grenadin de veau

vegetable oil - l'huile de végétale

vegetable oil from first pressing - l'huile de première pression

venison - le chevreuil

venison, haunch of - le gigot de chevreuil

verbena - la verveine

vinegar - le vinaigre

vinegar, balsamic - le vinaigre balsamique

vinegar, red wine - le vinaigre vin rouge

vinegar, white wine - le vinaigre vin blanc

W

walnut - la noix

walnut oil - l'huile de noix

watercress - le cresson

whitebait - la blanchaille

whiting - le merlan

wild boar - le sanglier

winkle - le bigorneau

woodcock - la bécasse

Y

yoghurt - le yaourt

Z

zucchini - la courgette

A to Z French to English

A

l'abricot – apricot

l'agneau – lamb

l'aiglefin - haddock

l'ail – garlic

l'aloyau – sirloin

la amande – almond

l'ananas – pineapple

l'anchois – anchovy

l' aneth - dill

l'anguille de roche – conger eel

l' anguille de sable – sand eel

l'artichaut - artichoke

l'asperges – asparagus

l'aubergine - aubergine (eggplant)

l'avocat - avocado

B

la banane – banana

le bar - sea bass

la barbue - brill

le basilic – basil

la bavette – undercut beef steak comes from the skirt

la bécasse – woodcock

la betterave rouge – beetroot

le beurre – butter

le beurre sale – salted butter

le beurre demi-sel – lightly salted butter

le beurre doux – unsalted butter

le bifteck/ steak – steak

le bigorneau - winkle

la blanchaille - whitebait

la blette - swiss chard

le boeuf - beef

le bouillon – stock cube

le bouillon de volaille - chicken stock

le boulgour - bulgar wheat

la brème - bream

le broccoli – broccoli

le brochet - pike

C

le cabillaud – cod

la cacahuète – peanut

la caille - quail

le canard – duck

le canette, la cane - duck (female)

la cannelle – cinnamon

la câpre – caper

la cardamome – cardamom

la carotte – carrot

le carrelet - plaice

le cassis – black currant

la cébette - spring onion

le céleri-en-branche – celery

le céleri-rave – celeriac

le cèpe – ceps or boletus mushroom

le cerfeuil – chervil

la cerise - cherry

la cervelle – brains

le champignon – mushroom

le chapon – capon

la châtaigne – small edible chestnut

le cheval – horse

le chevreuil - venison

le chou – cabbage

le chou-fleur – cauliflower

le chou frisé de Milan - savoy cabbage

le chou rouge - red cabbage

le chou- rave - kholrabi

la ciboulette – chives

le citron – lemon

le citron vert – lime

le clou de girofle – clove

le colin – hake

le collet - scrag (end) of lamb

le concombre – cucumber

la confiture – jam

le congre - conger eel

la coquille Saint-Jacques – scallop

le cornichon - gherkin

la côtelette – lamb chop / **lamb cutlet**

les côtes – loin chops

le coq - cockerel

le coquelet - cock (under 2lb)

le cou – neck

le cou de Bruxelles - Brussel sprout

la courge - squash

la courgette - courgette (zucchini)

le couscous – couscous

le crabe – crab

la crème – cream

le cresson - watercress

la crevette – prawn

le cul – tail

les cuisses – thighs

D

la daurade - gilt head bream

le dinde – turkey

E

l'échalote – shallot

l'echine – shoulder of pork or lamb

100

l'écrevisse – crayfish
l'églefin - haddock
l'encornet - squid
l'endive – chicory
l'entrecôte – ribeye
l'épeautre – spelt
les épinards – spinach
l'espadon - swordfish
l'estragon – tarragon
F
la faisan – pheasant
la farine – flour
la farine d'avoine – oatmeal flour
la farine de blé – wheat flour
la farine de châtaigne – chestnut flour
la farine de froment – wheat flour
la farine de maïs – cornflour
la farine de sarrasin – buckwheat flour
la farine de seigle – rye flour
la farine de riz – rice flour
le feneuil – fennel
les féves - broad beans
la figue – fig
le filet de porc - pork fillet
le filet de boef - beef fillet
le foie – liver
la fraise – strawberry
la framboise – raspberry
le fromage – cheese
le fromage de brebis - sheeps cheese
le fromage de chèvre - goats cheese
G
le gigot d'agneau - leg of lamb
le gigot de chevreuil - haunch of venison

le gingembre - ginger

le gîte (à la noix) - topside of beef

la glace - ice cream

la glace pile – crushed ice

la grenade – pomegranate

le grenadin de veau - veal medallion

la groseille - red currant

H

l'hareng - herring

le haricot vert - green bean / French bean

les haricots oeil de perdrix - black eyed peas

l'homard – lobster

l'huile d'arachide – peanut oil

l'huile de colza – rapeseed oil

l'huile de noix – walnut oil

l'huile d'olive – olive oil

l'huile de séseme – seseme oil

l'huile de tournesol – sunflower oil

l'huile de végétale – vegetable oil

l'huile de première pression – vegetable oil from first pressing

l'huile de viege – extra virgin – olive oil from first cold pressing

l'huître – oyster

l'hysope – hyssop

J

le jambon - ham

le jarret - lamb shank or shin

les joues – cheeks

L

le lait – milk

le lait écrémé – skimmed milk

le lait entire – full fat milkle yaourt – yoghurt

la laiture – lettuce

le lançon - sand eel

la langue de bœuf - beef tongue

la langoustine - langoustine - Dublin Bay prawn

le lapereau - rabbit (young)

le lapin – rabbit

le lardon – diced bacon

le laurier – bay (la feuille de laurier – bay leaf)

la lavande – lavender

les lentilles – lentils

le lieu jeune – pollack

le lièvre – hare

la limande-sole - lemon sole

le lingue julienne – ling

la lotte de mer – monkfish

M

la mâche - lambs lettuce

magret – breast

le mais – sweetcorn

le maquereau - mackerel

la marjolaine – marjoram

le marron – chestnut

la mayonnaise - mayonnaise

le melon – melon

le merlan – whiting

le merlu - hake

la merluche – dried cod

la menthe – mint

le merou – grouper

le miel – honey

la mirabelle - mirabelle plum

la morille – morel mushroom

la morue – cod

la moule – mussel

le moutarde – mustard

la mûre - blackberry

N

le navet – turnip

la noisette – hazelnut

la noix – walnut

la noix du Brésil - Brazil nut

la noix de coco - coconut

la noix de cajou - cashew nut

les nouilles - noodles

O

le oeuf – egg

l'olive - olive

l'oignon – onion

l'orange – orange

l'origan – oregano

l'orphie - garfish

l'os - bone

l'os à moelle - marrowbone

l'oseille - sorrel

P

la pacane – pecan

le padre - partridge

la palourde – clam

le pamplemousse – grapefruit

le paprika – paprika

les pâtes – pasta

les pâtes alimentaires – dried pasta

les pâtes frâiches – fresh pasta

les pâtes à potage – soup noodles

la pêche - peach

le persil – parsley

les petits pois – peas

le pigeonneau – squab

le pignon de pin – pine nut (pine kernel)

le piment – chilli pepper

la pintade - guinea hen

la pistache –pistachio

la pleurotte – oyster mushroom

la poire - pear

le poireau – leek

les pois chiches - chick peas

le poison - fish

le poisson-épée - swordfish

la poitrine – pork belly – bacon

la poitrine/ le poitrail – breast of lamb

le poivre – pepper

le poivron – pepper, capsicum

la pomme - apple

la pomme de terre - potato

le porc - pork

le potimarron - potimarron squash

le potiron - pumpkin

la poule – hen

le poulet - hen (young)

le poulet - chicken

le poulpe - octopus

le poussin – chick

la prune - plum

la purée de tomates - tomato puree

Q

le quinoa - quinoa

R

le radis - radish

le radis noir - black radish

le radis blanc - daikon radish or mooli

la raie - skate

le rasin - grape

le raisin sec – raisin

la réglisse – liquorice

la reine-claude - greengage

le requin - shark

la rhubarb - rhubarb

le riz - rice

la rocquette - rocket

le rognon - kidney

le romarin – rosemary

le romsteak/ le rumsteak - rump steak

le rouget - mullet

le rouget barbet - red mullet

le rouget de vase - striped mullet

le rouget grondin - gurnard

S

le saint-pierre - john dory

le sanglier – wild boar

la sardine – sardine

la sarriette – savory

le saumon – salmon

la saucisse - sausage (fresh or cooked)

le saucisson - sausage (dried)

la sauge – sage

la scarole - escarole (batavia)

la seiche – cuttlefish

la selle d'agneau – saddle of lamb

le serpolet - wild thyme

la sole - dover sole

le steak à hacher- steak for mincing

le sucre – sugar

le sucre cristallisé – granulated sugar

le sucre en poudre – caster sugar

le syrop de érable – maple syrup

T

le taureau - bull

la tête de veau - rolled veal head, including the tongue

le thon - tuna

le thon rouge - blue fin tuna

le thym – thyme

le tilleul - lime blossom (linden)

la tomate - tomato

la tomate cerise - cherry tomato

la tomate sechée - sundried tomato

le topinambour- jerusalem artichoke

le tournedos/ filet mignon – tenderloin beef or lamb steak

le tourteau = le crabe - crab

la tranche grasse – silverside of beef

la tranche – slice

le travers de porc - spare rib of pork

la truffe - truffle

la truite - trout

le turbot - turbot

V

le veau – veal

la verveine – verbena

viande avec l'os - meat on the bone

le vinaigre – vinegar

le vinaigre vin blanc – white wine vinegar

le vinaigre vin rouge – red wine vinegar

le vinaigre balsamique – balsamic vinegar

Y

le yaourt – yoghurt

le yaourt à la Grecque nature - Greek yoghurt

L - #0388 - 130423 - C0 - 210/148/6 - PB - DID3545755